ANIMAL CHAMPIONS OF THE JUNGLE

By Madeline Tyler

BookLife PUBLISHING

©2021
BookLife Publishing Ltd.
King's Lynn
Norfolk, PE30 4LS

All rights reserved.
Printed in Malta.

A catalogue record for this book is available from the British Library.

ISBN: 978-1-83927-449-7

Written by:
Madeline Tyler

Edited by:
Emilie Dufresne

Designed by:
Drue Rintoul

All facts, statistics, web addresses and URLs in this book were verified as valid and accurate at time of writing. No responsibility for any changes to external websites or references can be accepted by either the author or publisher.

Photo Credits

All images are courtesy of Shutterstock.com. With thanks to Getty Images, Thinkstock Photo and iStockphoto. Throughout – Cocos. Bounty. Front Cover&1 – apple2499, CWIS, Anan Kaewkhammul, Milan M, Elnur. 2–3 – Teo Tarras, PRANEE JIRAKITDACHAKUN. 4–5 – Cristi Popescu, Ondrej Prosicky. 6–7 – Frank McClintock, Damsea, nattanan726. 8–9 – Atthapol Saita, Glenn Young, Enrique Aguirre, Travel Stock. 10–11 – jeep2499, Daniel_Ferryanto, Sanit Fuangnakhon. 12–13 – Jukka Jantunen, Shutterranger. 14–15 – mark higgins, Misbachul Munir, LeonP. 16–17 – Jonah Goh, Andreas Gradin, nattanan726. 18–19 – LABETAA Andre, Patrick K. Campbell, SachinSubran. 20–21 – Jiri Hrebicek, Eric Isselee, Marc Lechanteur, Vladimir Wrangel. 22–23 – Lori Jaeski, Purino, Darren Baker, Denis Kuvaev.

CONTENTS

Page 4   In the Jungle
Page 5   What Makes an Animal Champion?
Page 6   Three-Toed Sloth
Page 8   Jaguar
Page 10   Orangutan
Page 12   African Forest Elephant
Page 14   Chimpanzee
Page 16   Malayan Tapir
Page 18   Green Anaconda
Page 20   Okapi
Page 22   Becoming a Champion
Page 24   Glossary and Index

Words that look like this can be found in the glossary on page 24.

IN THE JUNGLE

Jungles are <u>tropical</u> forests. They are very hot and very wet. Some animals live at the tops of the trees, some animals live on the jungle floor, and some animals live somewhere in between!

Let's meet the **animal champions** that call the jungle their home!

WHAT MAKES AN ANIMAL CHAMPION?

Animal champions don't always have to be the biggest, fastest, or strongest animals around. They are champions because of the adaptations they have, or things they can do.

Come on! Let's head into the jungle...

THREE-TOED SLOTH

Sloths move so slowly that <u>algae</u> grows on them. This may not sound good, but it helps them <u>camouflage</u> against the green trees of the jungle.

Sloths are some of the slowest animals on Earth!

Champion of Camouflage

Sloths spend most of their lives up in the trees. Their long claws help them to hold onto branches.

Sloths can even sleep while holding onto trees. This is useful because they can spend up to 20 hours a day sleeping!

Champion of Long Naps

JAGUAR

You may think that most cats are afraid of water, but these big cats love swimming. Jaguars are very good swimmers, and they use this skill to hunt fish.

Champion of the Big Bite

Caiman

Jaguars have very strong teeth – they can bite through caimans and turtle shells!

Jaguars are also great at climbing trees. There are lots of trees in the jungle, so jaguars can climb up high to hide and to hunt.

Champion of Climbing High

Jaguars hunt during the day and at night.

ORANGUTAN

The orangutan is the largest arboreal <u>mammal</u>. Orangutans spend most of their time in trees, and their long, strong arms make it easy to swing from branch to branch.

Champion of Strong Swings

Arboreal animals are animals that live in trees.

Orangutans are very clever and are closely <u>related</u> to humans. They stay dry in the wet jungle by making nests within the trees and using leaves as umbrellas.

Champion of Staying Dry

Orangutan means 'person of the forest' in a language called Malay.

11

AFRICAN FOREST ELEPHANT

It can sometimes be hard to spot African forest elephants, so scientists <u>estimate</u> how many elephants there are by counting their poos!

African forest elephants are smaller than African savannah elephants, but they are very closely related.

The poo of African forest elephants is very important for helping the rainforest grow. Some trees grow better when an African forest elephant eats their seeds and then poos them out!

Champion of Pooing!

CHIMPANZEE

Chimpanzees are very clever animals. They use sticks and branches to get insects from inside trees and logs. This means they can get to food that some other animals may not be able to find.

They also use stones, roots and wood to crack hard nuts open.

Champion of Clever Eating

There are lots of deadly animals and plants in the jungle. To stay safe and not get hurt, chimpanzees use sticks to move and look at dead snakes and other things that could be dangerous.

Champion of Using Tools

A tool is a thing you use to help you do something.

15

MALAYAN TAPIR

Malayan tapirs have a very good sense of smell. They wee on jungle pathways so that other Malayan tapirs can sniff it and find their way to feeding and drinking areas.

Champion of Sniffing out Smells

Swimming is a great way to cool off in the hot jungle, and tapirs are very good at it! They also like to wallow in the mud, which might also be a way of getting rid of ticks.

Champion of Keeping Cool

Their snouts are good for smelling, but they also use them as a snorkel while swimming underwater.

GREEN ANACONDA

Green anacondas are very good hunters. They are mostly nocturnal, which means they sleep during the day but are awake and hunt at night. This means it is harder for them to be seen.

Champion of Hunting at Night

Green anacondas are the heaviest snakes in the world.

A green anaconda's eyes and nostrils are on the top of its head. This allows it to hide underwater and wait for <u>prey</u> to come by, before taking it by surprise and attacking!

Nostril

Eye

Champion of the Surprise Attack

OKAPI

Okapis have fur that is perfect for the jungle. It's very oily, so the water slides right off it, just like a raincoat. This keeps them dry on rainy days.

Champion of Not Getting Wet

Okapis have long tongues that are great for grabbing and holding food. An okapi uses its tongue to pull leaves off trees and put them into its mouth.

Champion of the Toughest Tongue

BECOMING A CHAMPION

Let's see what animal adaptations we humans can use to be champions of the jungle!

Face paint and camouflaged clothes will help you hide like a sloth.

Shoes with good grip will help you climb like a jaguar.

Goggles and a snorkel will help you swim like a green anaconda.

A raincoat will keep you dry like an okapi.

23

GLOSSARY

adaptations changes that have happened to an animal over time and help them to be better suited to their environment
algae a plant or plant-like living thing that has no roots, stems, leaves or flowers
camouflage traits that allow an animal to hide itself in a habitat
estimate make a careful guess
mammal an animal that has warm blood, a backbone and produces milk
prey animals that are hunted by other animals for food
related connected or part of the same family group
ticks small animals that attach themselves to people and other animals and suck their blood
tropical a hot and humid area or place
wallow roll in

INDEX

branches 7, 10, 14
camouflage 6, 22
climbing 9, 22
fur 20
poo 12–13
seeds 13
sleeping 7, 18
snorkels 17, 23
swimming 8, 17, 23
teeth 8
tongues 21
trees 4, 6–7, 9–11, 13–14, 21
wee 16